The Patriot Game

The Patriot Game

Roswell Angier

Norman Hurst

David R. Godine, Publisher · Boston

With special appreciation to Donald Patterson, who originated
the idea for this project.

First published in 1975 by
David R. Godine, Publisher
306 Dartmouth Street
Boston, Massachusetts

Printed in the United States of America

THE PATRIOT GAME is an attempt to document how contemporary Americans relate to the monuments and events of a common past, what the history texts call a 'heritage.' It is not simply about the exercise of patriotism.

The photographs were made at various patriotic ceremonies in Boston, and also along a four-mile pedestrian route, marked off in red on the city's pavement, which is punctuated by historical landmarks: Granary Burying Ground, Old South Meeting House, the site of the Boston Massacre, Faneuil Hall, Paul Revere's House, Old North Church, and others. This route is called the Freedom Trail. Its setting is typically urban, though the monuments which define it make it Boston's major tourist attraction.

The text which accompanies the photographs was gathered from interviews and public addresses, both along the Freedom Trail and at patriotic observances in Boston. From the fervent contemporary pilgrim to the merely happenstance witness, the people whose words we have used reflect a broad range of feelings about the past, and their relation to it.

Roswell Angier
Norman Hurst
Cambridge, Massachusetts, 1975

There are all different kinds of people come in here. Of course, anybody that would climb all those damn stairs is interested. But I have had people — we see it practically every day at this time of year — they will come in, walk to the center of the hall, turn around, and walk out. They've been to Faneuil Hall. That's all. They just want to check it off as another place they have been to.

Conversely, two or three years ago, I saw an old fellow standing out there, and when I say old, I mean he was over seventy-five, and he stood there and just looked around and looked around. Along after, I spoke to him. He says, 'You know, I never thought I'd live to see this day.'

That was the most important thing to him, to come to Faneuil Hall. He'd been thinking of it for forty years. So, you get the two extremes. But the average person who comes in here is pretty interested. As I say, he has to be, to climb up those stairs.

Curator, Faneuil Hall Armory

We were wondering what came after '75.

What came after '75. . .'76?

That's the spirit!

Spectators

What happens after '75 and '76? Right down the drain again. Right?

Militiaman

What really bothers me is 'The Spirit of '76.' You know, the picture. The drummer, the guy carrying the flag, the thing's a joke. That thirteen-star flag wasn't turned out to the public until July 4, 1777, and yet it's called 'The Spirit of '76.' How can that be? Bunker Hill goes back to '75. The only thing that happened in '76 of any notable popularity was the signing of the Declaration of Independence.

A Charlestown Militiaman

People who come here are amazed. They're amazed at how big the original colony was; they're amazed at the extent of Massachusetts; they're amazed at how few people, like Sam Adams and Jefferson and Hancock and John Adams, wanted the complete break that no one else did; they are amazed at how far-seeing and how far-sighted these men were, those few who kept pressing for the complete break in the Declaration.

They are amazed that people would charge money for fighting at Concord or for riding a horse. They are amazed that Revere would turn the Massacre into such a propaganda thing. They are amazed to hear the things that went on behind the scenes, such as the taking of the vote for the Constitution and the renaming of the state. They are just amazed at the gimmicks, I guess.

Guide, State Archive

Oh, those hats, those awful hats! They're made out of . . . they're not even made of felt. What are they made out of? The three cornered ones? Have you been in our gift shop? It's sort of embarrassing.

We sell a cat's head, which is a sort of chipped away wooden cat's head on a plaque, which is supposedly what they have at the front of ships or the back of ships or something. Forty dollars. They're this big! The man who made it just sat down and chiseled for half an hour. We really sold one the other day, which was the occasion of much rejoicing all around . . . and much disbelief.

They don't buy the nice things. I'm going to buy some things, though, to take home anyway. Things like tea saying 'from the Boston Tea Party' seems to me a rather nice thing to have; but nobody gets that.

The funniest thing is to try and get people from Boston at the Old State House. You say, 'Would you like to visit the Boston Tea Party Ship and Museum?'

They say, 'Aw no, I'm from Bawston. I don't have to see it.'

You say, 'If you haven't seen it, wouldn't you like to go and see it?'

And they say, 'Aw, no, I'm from Bawston. I don't have to.'

You say, 'Why? Because I've asked?' You know they don't want to be thought of as a tourist.

Boston Tea Party Ship Employee

How come there are pews in here? Is this a church?

Why couldn't they meet in the Granary?

Maybe it was filled with grain.

It is a bit strange that the whole population could have gotten into Old South.

It makes the Revolution look like a minority movement.

Well, the population was probably about twenty-five, thirty thousand, and half of them were women. That cuts it down a bit. I don't imagine they let slaves in, either.

Did the population include slaves?

There's Lafayette, America's darling!

He was real young, wasn't he?

Yeah, a real answer to a teenager's prayer.

There's a picture of George III, he was real ugly.

Did you see those old wooden shoes over there? They look just like my pair of Dr. Scholls.

I have a piece of the tree where George Washington stood, when he commanded the army!

A piece of the tree, Jesus!

Visitors at Old South Meeting House

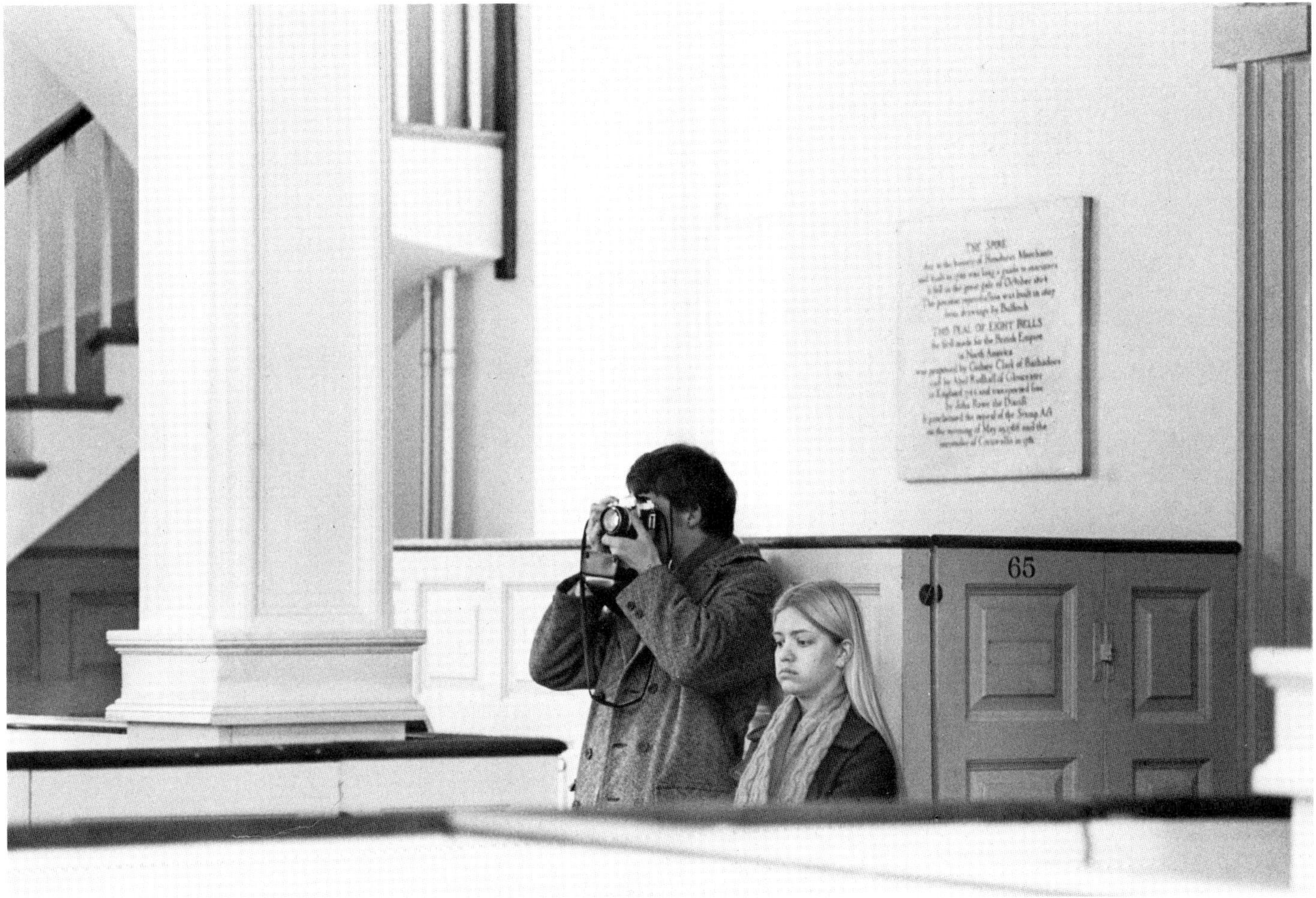
65

I have to represent the War Mothers. They asked me to come. It's for the first black man. First man that was killed in the Revolution was a black man. They was four, five of 'em killed. The first five colored men. They were all buried over here at Granary Cemetery together. It's a big day for them people.

Well, it's quite an honor, the colored people think, that the first man that was killed in the American Revolution was a black man. And four of 'em other colored men were. And they were shot right here where the bandstand is. Crispus Attucks, there is a book on it, 'The First Man to Die.' I read it.

He went to fight the men; and he had no gun, and they had guns. He had kind of like a whip in his hand. They shot him down. The book is grand. It was written by a man from Swampscott. Quite a book. I read it.

I didn't know half about the American Revolution. I thought I was versed, but I didn't know half til I read the book. Maybe when you go to school you learn that stuff, American history; but I'd forgotten it, I guess, or I didn't learn it.

Representative, War Mothers of New England

I've had a hard time dealing with the whole issue of Crispus Attucks. What happened to Crispus Attucks was that he got shot, and those other guys got shot, but they all got caught up in this big propaganda movement that Sam Adams was running. So that event became a **massacre**, right? That was a PR thing. There's nothing wrong with that, but Crispus Attucks wasn't the first person who got killed in the American Revolution, because that was not the American Revolution. The reason we remember Crispus Attucks' name is because of the people who decided to make that event a massacre, and used that event to arouse people in this colony. They won, eventually. And since they won, we remember their names.

But it really was a riot. And it really wasn't that much different from the overreaction of cops in Newark, or New York, or Detroit, but we can't remember the names of the black people who were shot in the '60's, the black people who are dead. That's because we didn't win. And if we do win, all those names will be dug out.

The important thing about Crispus Attucks is not to make him into a big-time hero. The important thing is just to say that there were black people all around the city. It wasn't unusual for a black person to be there and get shot. It wasn't unusual for black people to be walking around State Street.

We try to talk about black people who we're sure made conscious decisions to fight in the American Revolution, like Peter Salem, whose rifle got stolen from the Bunker Hill monument. Also, we talk about the fact that a lot of black people didn't fight on the American side. The British offered black people freedom, if they fought with them, before Washington did.

Spokesman for the Museum of Afro-American History

George Washington was a real prick, he was a real son of a bitch. I don't doubt the man was gifted, he had some kind of gift to him. He had to be a gifted guy; because if you look at his coat in the Smithsonian Institute, he's got bullet-holes in his coat, seven different holes, and two of them are almost point-blank in his heart. Never once did one of those balls touch his skin. He always led his men in a battle, and never once was he even scratched.

Plus he's supposed to have seen the Indian, what's his name? Potomac? The Indian who predicted the Civil War, another war, would happen in a hundred years. He talked to the Indian the night before the march on Trenton, before they crossed the Delaware on Christmas eve, and the Indian told him to make this march. For a guy to predict that, almost a hundred years before, there's got to be something to him. Good old dirty George. I think there was more to Betsy Ross than her sewing.

A Colonial Militiaman

How many times a day does that get thrown in the water?

I don't know, I'm only here in the afternoon, but I should think two hundred and fifty, towards three hundred. Originally they had over three hundred chests, so it's, you know, the same amount of splashes.

Guide

Well, I think the very fact that they're tourists, that they felt like coming here identifies them as having some feeling. Or maybe they want to say, 'at least we're here.' They must have some feeling for it or they wouldn't have made the trip. I think it's a pilgrimage, like to Mecca. Why do you go there? Because it's there! You know, like the mountain. Ha, ha, ha! I don't know.

Parishioner, Christ Church

His house is right down the street there. Paul Revere's house. It's the oldest wooden structure.

I revere Paul Revere: he got caught right off. The other guy made it.

He got caught? Revere?

Sure, he was caught before he even got out of Boston. The rest was all just patriotic fancy. He got caught right off. It was the other guys that got through and warned everyone. For some reason they, ah, revere him.

Visitors to Paul Revere Mall

American history books are written by racists. That's one thing. The other problem is that they're written by elitists. People mostly learn about 5% of the population — the crazy idea that these guys are the fathers of our country. They may be the fathers of our country, but they're not the fathers of **us**. And they're not the fathers of the average white person who goes on the Freedom Trail. They're not related to those people. And what were **their** ancestors doing?

A Black Civic Leader

It is, I believe, important for us to be here. Reenactments, celebrations, memorials are important and essential if we are to acknowledge the fact that we exist as a community; because no community, no people, no nation long survives without the support of ritual acts, the celebration of what, and who, and why we are.

Without it, the psyche of a people withers. It loses all sense of identity, it loses the very marrow of existence. In this annual commemoration, we gather here and lift up the meaning of our life together. We lift up our mutual anguish in our divisions here, and in our island world. Here and now, we affirm that it is in celebration that we are transformed, renewed, and given a heart of flesh, made a new people, a new creation, given a new strength and vision, to make a world for us, a brand new world for us — a world in which people will do justly, love mercy, and walk humbly with God and with each other, somehow, someday, somewhere.

Vicar, Christ Church
Boston Massacre Commemoration

We're very historical here. And we're in the most historical part of the United States. Bunker Hill Day. This is where it all began, fella! Here, and at Lexington and Concord.

You know, if there was never a Battle of Bunker Hill, there might not have been fifty states. You might have been an Englishman, and I might have been an Englishman! And God forgive me, I'm an Irishman!

Member, Veterans Organization, Charlestown

I think it's a great thing to celebrate, to remember. But I think it's been glamorized and we're remembering all the good things and none of the bad things. . . .

Such as an angry mob harrassing people, terrifying the British soldiers, such as no command was ever given to fire! And, I think you should also recall that John Adams defended the soldiers and got them acquitted. He felt that they were not guilty.

If you stand here long enough she is going to liken it to Kent State. She's a Tory.

Three Members of a Colonial Women's Organization
Boston Massacre Exercises

It's always an amusing thing in Old North Church when the kid supposedly
carries the lanterns up the stairs. Every April 18th evening, or whatever the day
is that they celebrate it, they get this six or eight year old, usually he's some
descendant of Paul Revere, to carry the two lanterns. He takes them as far as the
entrance to the tower stairs, and they photograph him on the stairs. And then the
guy just goes over and flips on the switches, and these two electric lanterns come
on in the steeple. It's just a hoax. They give him about 15 seconds or so to have
climbed the stairs and then snap on the lights . . . ha, ha, ha . . . that's the
Twentieth Century for you.

Local Photographer

Let's face it. If we hadn't 'a won the war, they'd have all been bums. They were
heroes because we won; they would have been bums if we'd lost. That's how
war or revolution goes. The winners are the heroes; the others are, you know,
the jerks.

Member, Colonial Organization

There it is, ladies and gentlemen, you're seeing it as it actually happened! [gunfire] The British stood fast in the face of continued volleys of patriot rebel firing [gunfire] standing bravely, as the British soldier was taught to do, in defiance!
There they are! [gunfire]
The patriot answer to the strong militant! [gunfire]
Another volley! [gunfire]
And there's the answer from the patriots! [gunfire] Never will we move from the hill! That is the cry, [gunfire] this is the answer! [gunfire] No sir, liberty at any price, that's the answer! There's the picture as it looked in 1775! [gunfire] This is the answer they give to the British redcoat, the lobster-back, the hated enemy!
Here they come, ladies and gentlemen, listen carefully, and watch these men as they march, standfast and straight, in defiance, into the muzzle of the patriot, this is exactly the way it happened! [gunfire] History is about to be recorded!

Announcer, Bunker Hill Reenactment

We have a lot of history in the city of Boston; we have a lot of things in the city of Boston; we have a lot of things in Massachusetts; and we have a lot of things in the country today that are good. Things are not too good in the country today, so a lot of people think, but I think that those who are in public life respect our history.

I will close by asking the media here in the city of Boston: sometimes we get at each other; sometimes we're critical of one another; but when you have something like this and when you have people who will come out to it, to respect the battle of Bunker Hill, that's the kind of media I'd like to have reported. Not the type that disrespects everything that exists; not the type that want to tear the country apart within. The sooner you ignore them the better off we're going to have us a wonderful country.

Boston City Councilman
Bunker Hill Day Patriotic Exercises

This is Independence Day. Raising the Flag is very important. It's to show the Americans who the Americans are. The Americans that are real Americans appreciate that.

I love to watch the parades when they're all in red, white, and blue. It's very pretty. It's an honor to watch them, it's an honor. I'm watching the kids do their dance there and one of them dropped the damn baton four times. I like to march! Too bad I'm not a man! Ha ha!

Onlooker

What's tonight?

Well, Boston Massacre. The two hundred an' fourth year.

What's gonna happen?

A little talk, an' a little march up to the graves, the sites, a little layin' of wreaths. Commemoration type of deal, ya know?

We did the reenactment . . . four years ago . . . of the two hundredth year. Yeah, we reenacted right here in Dock Square. We had the red coats out. We did all the yellin' and the hollerin' and all that shit, like they did. And now it's a commemoration. Two hundred and four years. Seventeen seventy, and now it's nineteen seventy-four. Two hundred and four years.

Member, Colonial Militia Group

The Longfellow poem is an interesting pervasive myth, the material out of which the civic religion is made. Of course, he gave this place the designation 'The Old North Church' because it fitted his metrical scheme, but you see how pervasive that is.

Everybody refers to the building as 'Old North Church', and that has never been its name. It is, and has always been, the charter of the church is: Christ Church in the City of Boston in New England. You see, 'Old North' disguises the fact that it is an Episcopal church, and it fits into the kind of broad Protestant mythos.

It's a very peculiar thing. This spot seems to be . . . I mean, here you're treading on sacred soil, the civic religion's high altar. I mean, people who worship the Flag as the central thing, 'My Country, right or wrong,' vaguely think that God's out there somewhere; but the important thing is that this is God's country. He's a nice guy because this is His country. That's what I mean by civic religion.

Yes, people have sort of a vague . . . a sort of a Protestant ethos, and they're really not Christians at all. They're pagans. They do know that the best nation in the world is the U.S. of A. The U.S. of A. does everything right and everyone else is a dirty foreigner and does things wrong. That's what I call the civic religion, that they are the chosen people and that the rest of the world is gentile.

Today I compared the plight of the British troops here at the time of the Revolution with our men in Vietnam. A man came up, an Army officer, and said, 'I resented very much your making that comparison!'

I said, 'Well, it's an inevitable comparison. And you're an Army officer aren't you?'

'Yes,' he said.

'Then, sir,' I said, 'you've sworn an oath to uphold the Constitution, which makes it my privilege to say what I think, sir. You defend me in my right to do that.'

Clergyman, Christ Church

THE PATRIOT GAME was designed by Roswell Angier, Norman Hurst, and Carol Goldenberg. The photography was reproduced by Halliday Lithograph Corporation in Hanover, Massachusetts. The text type, Stymie Medium, was set at the Monotype Composition Company, Boston, Massachusetts. The books were printed on Monadnock Astrolite and bound by the New Hampshire Bindery.